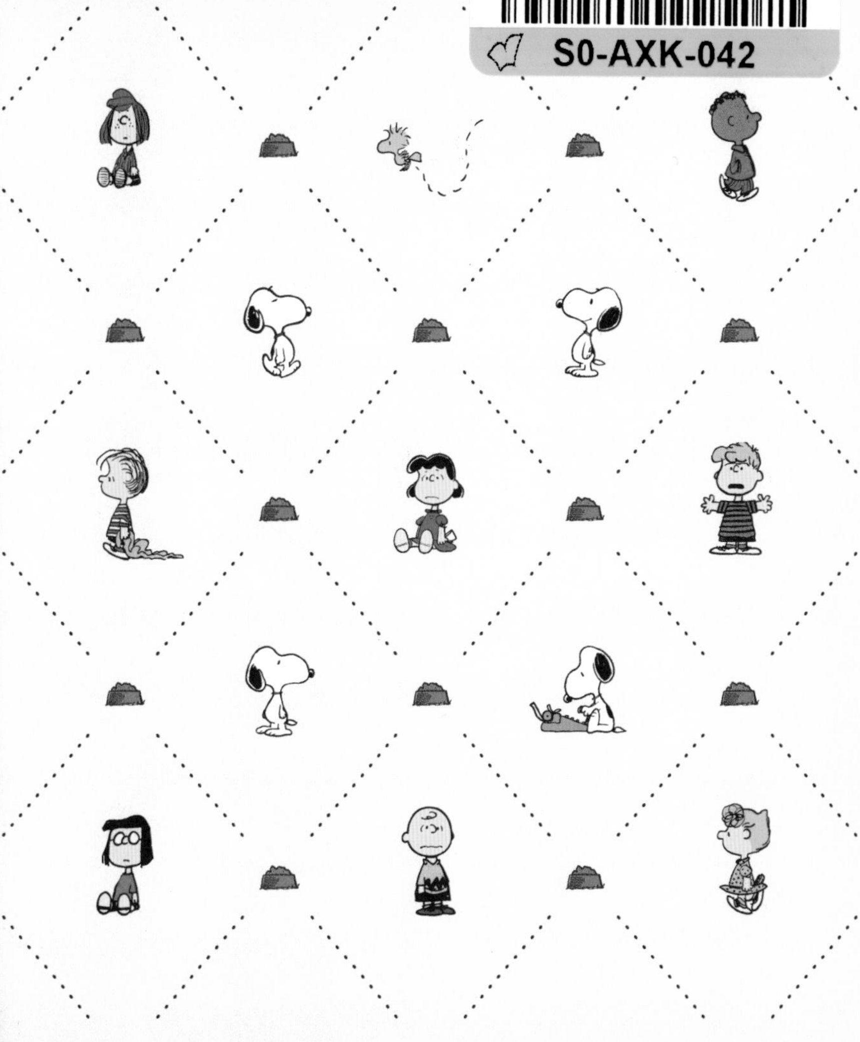

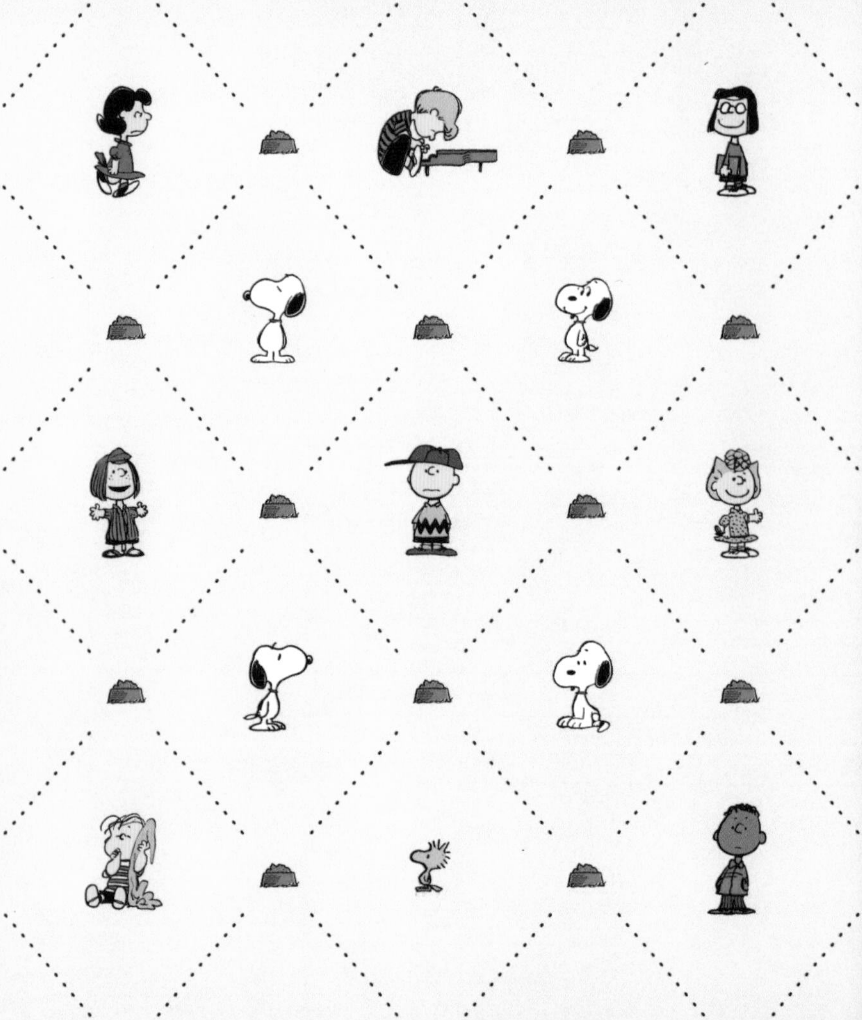

Running Press
Hachette Book Group
1290 Avenue of the Americas, New York, NY 10104
www.runningpress.com
@Running_Press

Printed in China

Originally published in 2014 by Canongate Books Ltd in the U.K.
First U.S. Edition: March 2018

Published by Running Press,
an imprint of Perseus Books, LLC,
a subsidiary of Hachette Book Group, Inc.
The Running Press name and logo is a trademark of the Hachette Book Group.

The publisher is not responsible for websites (or their content)
that are not owned by the publisher.

Print book cover and interior design by Rafaela Romaya and layout by Stuart Polson.

www.peanuts.com

Library of Congress Control Number: 2017942495

ISBN: 978-0-7624-6354-1

LREX

10 9 8 7 6 5 4 3 2 1

THE PHILOSOPHY OF
SNOOPY

CHARLES M. SCHULZ

Running Press

PHILADELPHIA

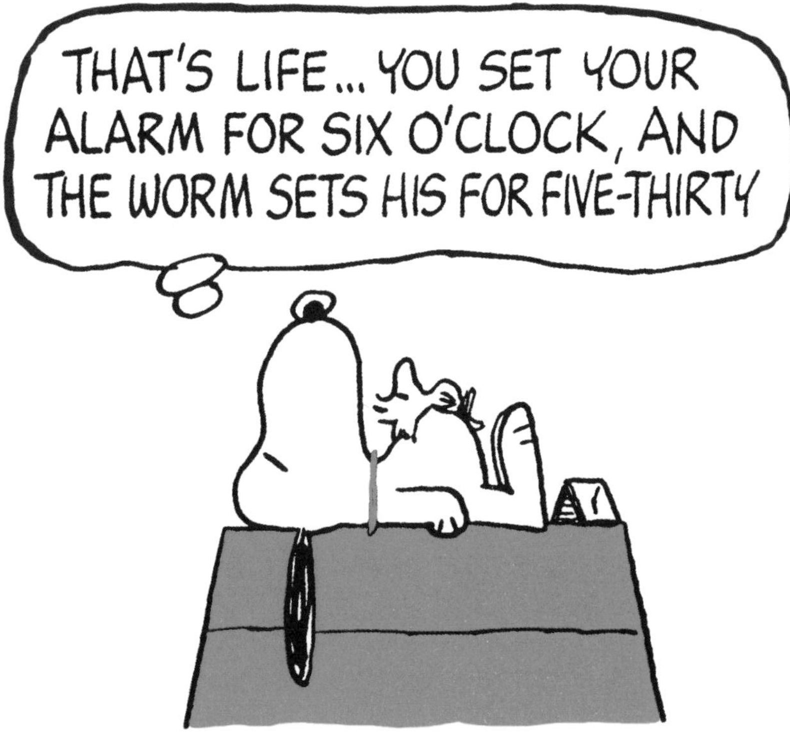
THAT'S LIFE... YOU SET YOUR ALARM FOR SIX O'CLOCK, AND THE WORM SETS HIS FOR FIVE-THIRTY

IT LOOKS LIKE TOMORROW WILL BE ANOTHER NICE DAY...
"RED AT NIGHT, SAILOR'S DELIGHT.. RED IN THE MORNING, SAILORS TAKE WARNING"
RED AT NOON... FLY A BALLOON
HEE HEE
RED AT TEN... A BIG FAT HEN!
HEE HEE HEE HEE

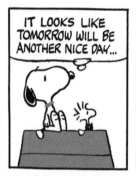

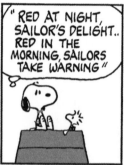

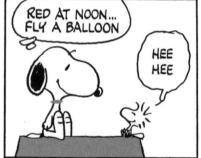

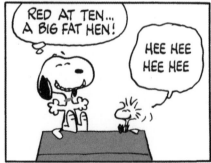

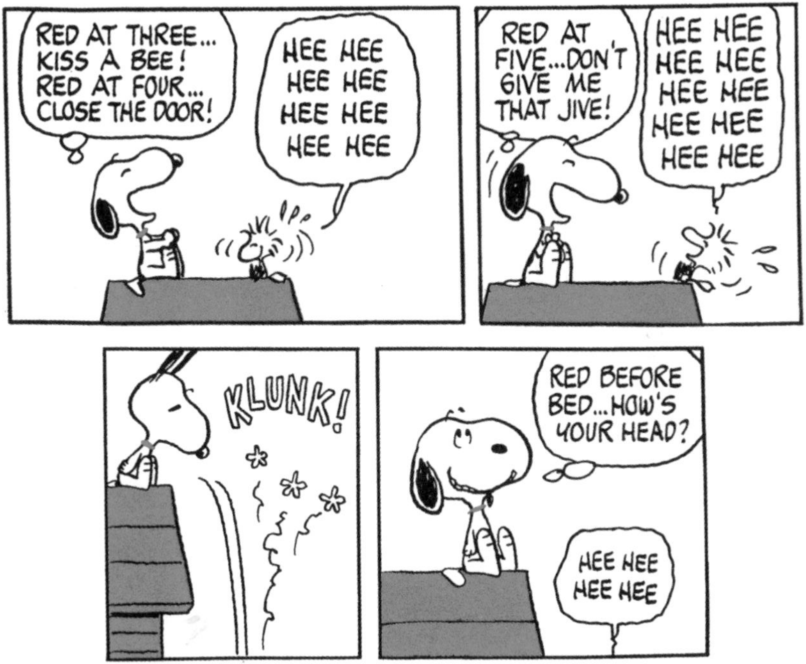
RED AT THREE... KISS A BEE! RED AT FOUR... CLOSE THE DOOR!
HEE HEE HEE HEE HEE HEE HEE HEE
RED AT FIVE...DON'T GIVE ME THAT JIVE!
HEE HEE HEE HEE HEE HEE HEE HEE HEE HEE
KLUNK!
RED BEFORE BED...HOW'S YOUR HEAD?
HEE HEE HEE HEE

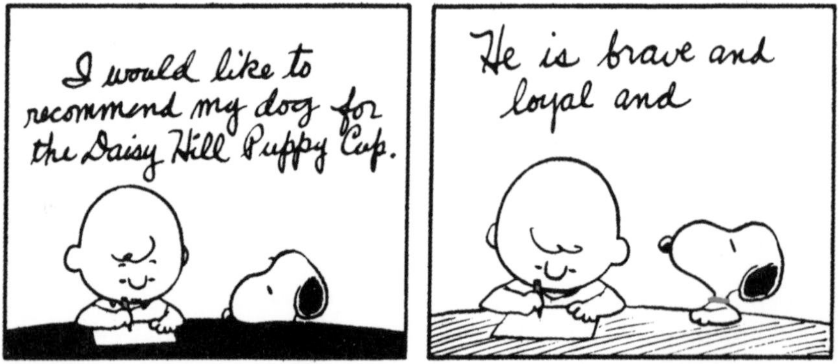
I would like to recommend my dog for the Daisy Hill Puppy Cup.
He is brave and loyal and

SNAP
SNAP
impatient

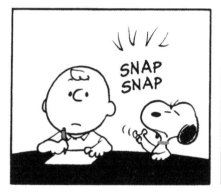

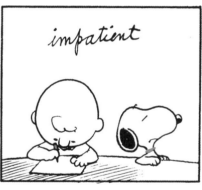

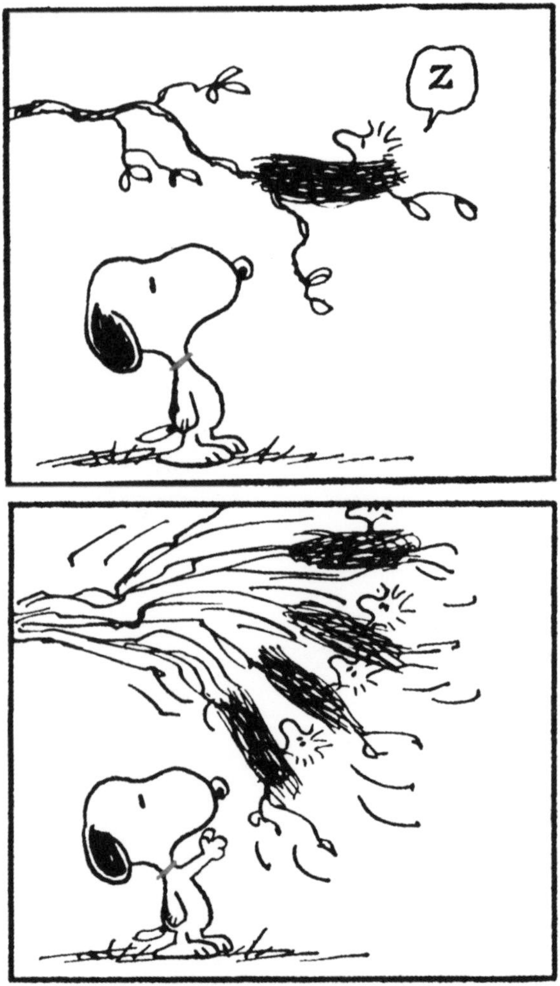
Z

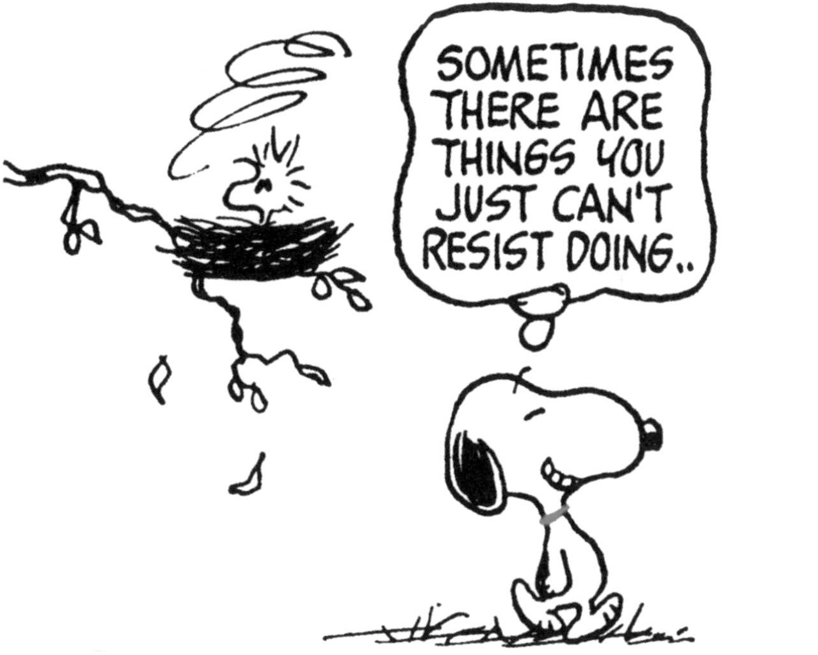
SOMETIMES THERE ARE THINGS YOU JUST CAN'T RESIST DOING..

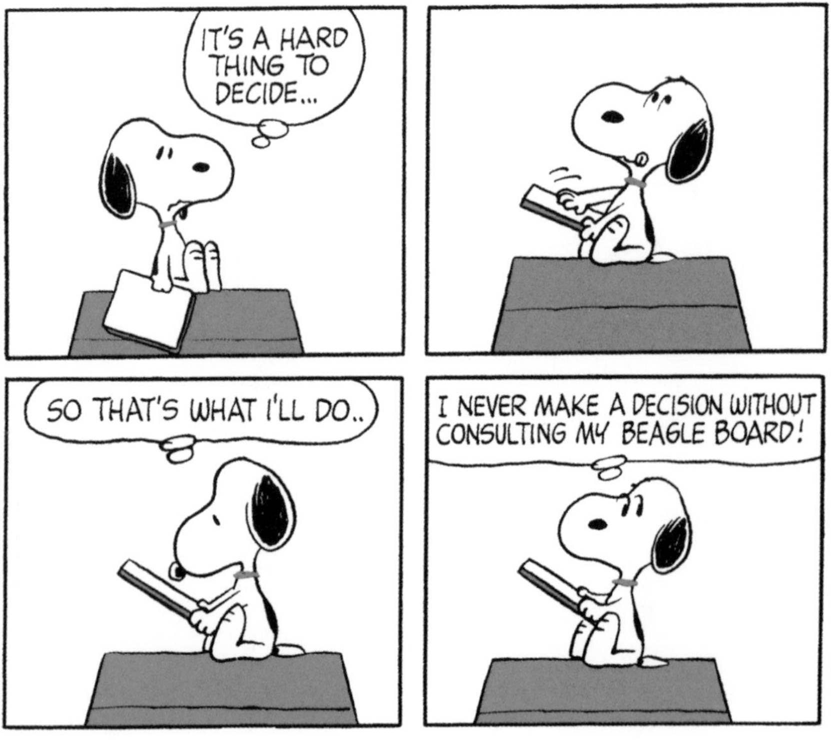
IT'S A HARD THING TO DECIDE...
SO THAT'S WHAT I'LL DO..
I NEVER MAKE A DECISION WITHOUT CONSULTING MY BEAGLE BOARD!

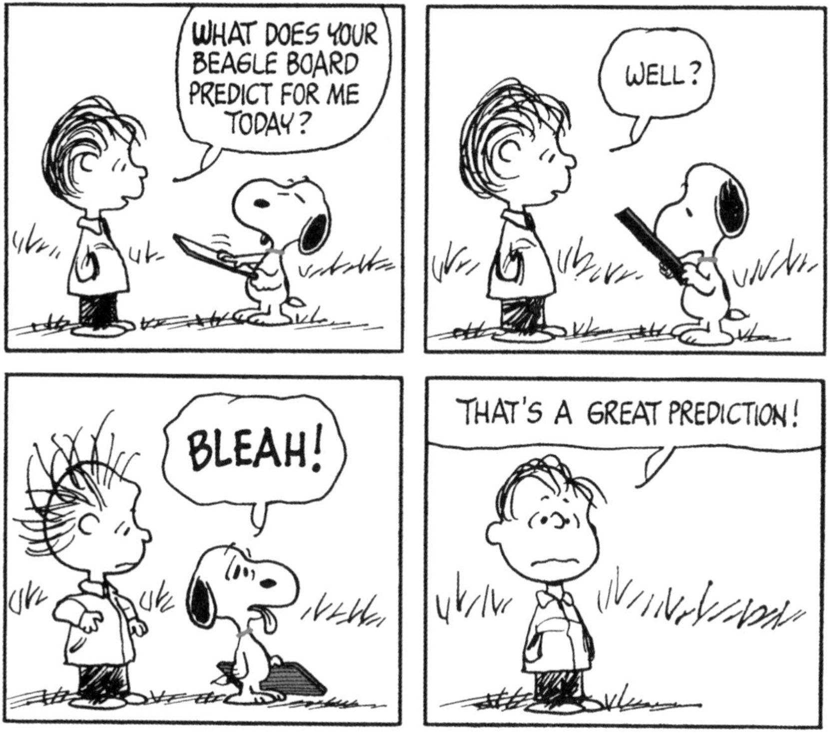
WHAT DOES YOUR BEAGLE BOARD PREDICT FOR ME TODAY?
WELL?
BLEAH!
THAT'S A GREAT PREDICTION!

NEVER SHARE YOUR PAD WITH A RESTLESS BIRD!

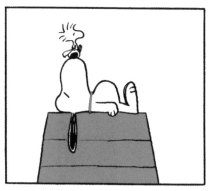

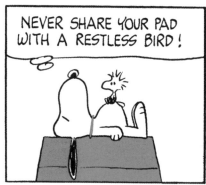

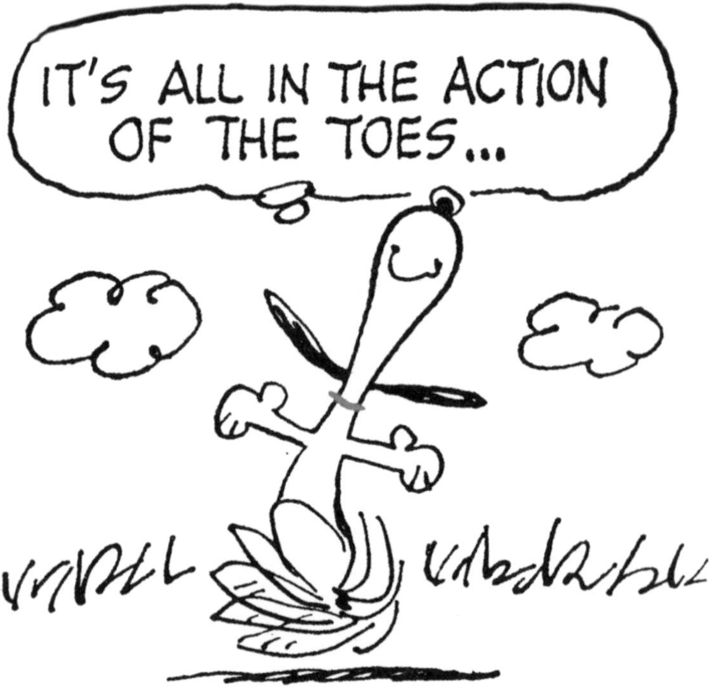
IT'S ALL IN THE ACTION OF THE TOES...

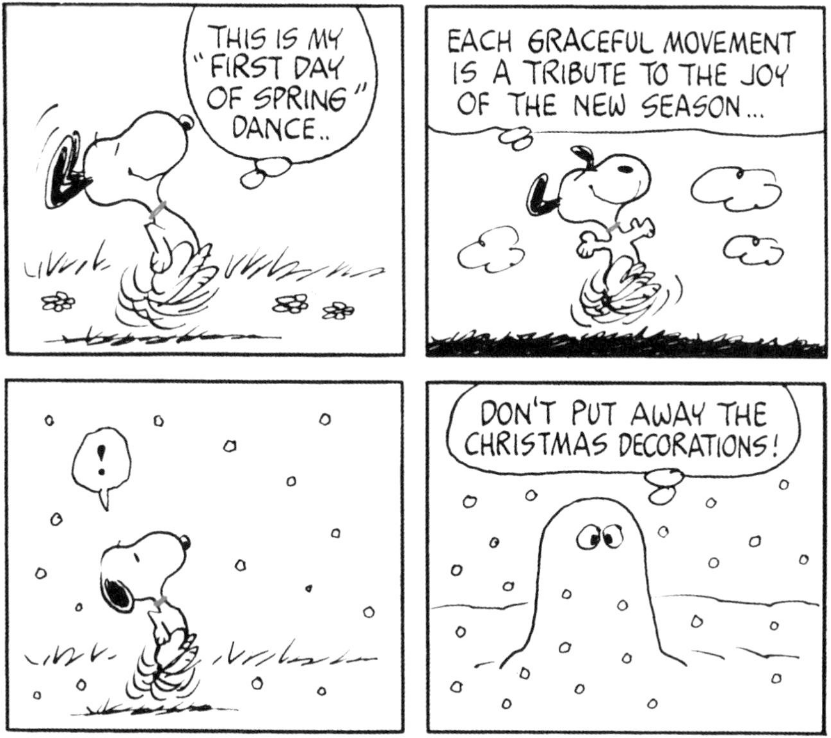
THIS IS MY "FIRST DAY OF SPRING" DANCE..
EACH GRACEFUL MOVEMENT IS A TRIBUTE TO THE JOY OF THE NEW SEASON...
!
DON'T PUT AWAY THE CHRISTMAS DECORATIONS!

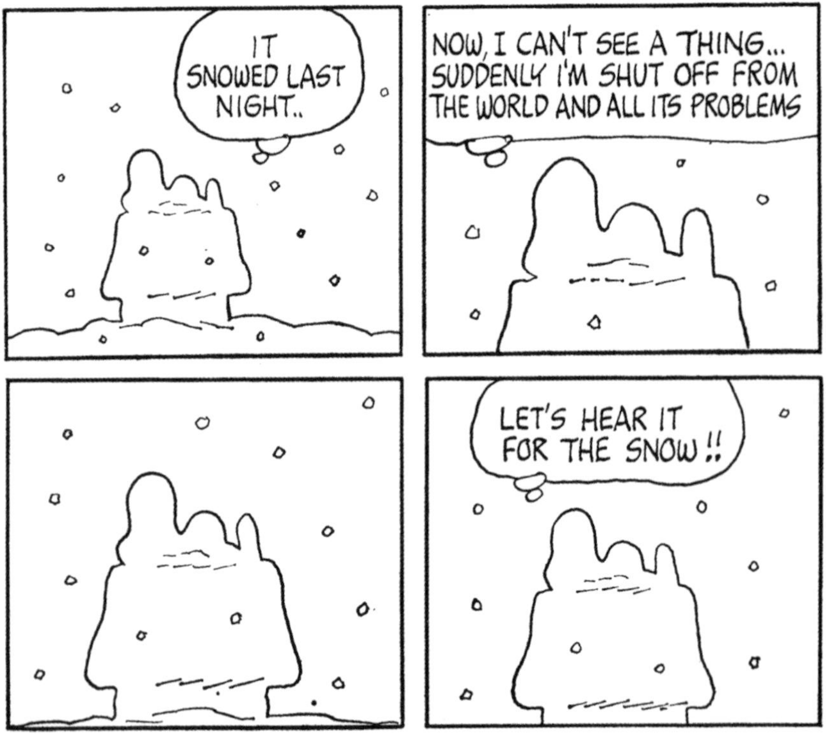
IT SNOWED LAST NIGHT..
NOW, I CAN'T SEE A THING... SUDDENLY I'M SHUT OFF FROM THE WORLD AND ALL ITS PROBLEMS
LET'S HEAR IT FOR THE SNOW!!

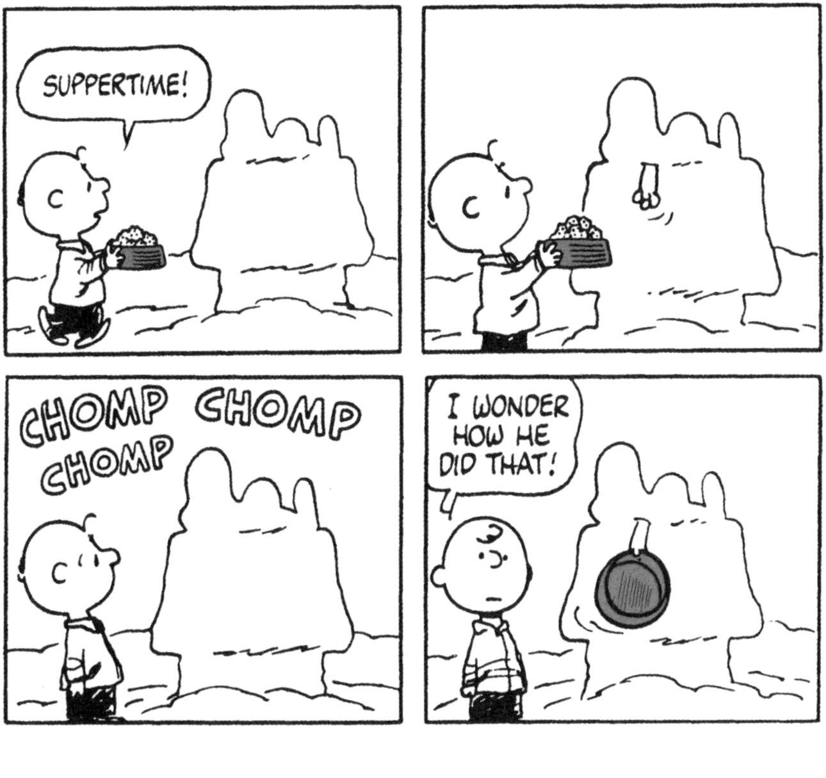
SUPPERTIME!
CHOMP CHOMP CHOMP
I WONDER HOW HE DID THAT!

SIGH
I SEARCH THE SKIES, BUT I CAN FIND NO MEANING!
NO MEANING!

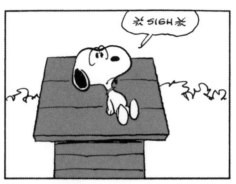

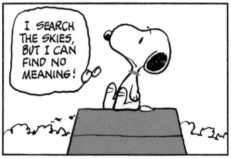

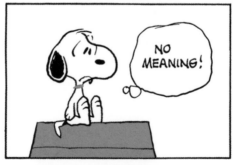

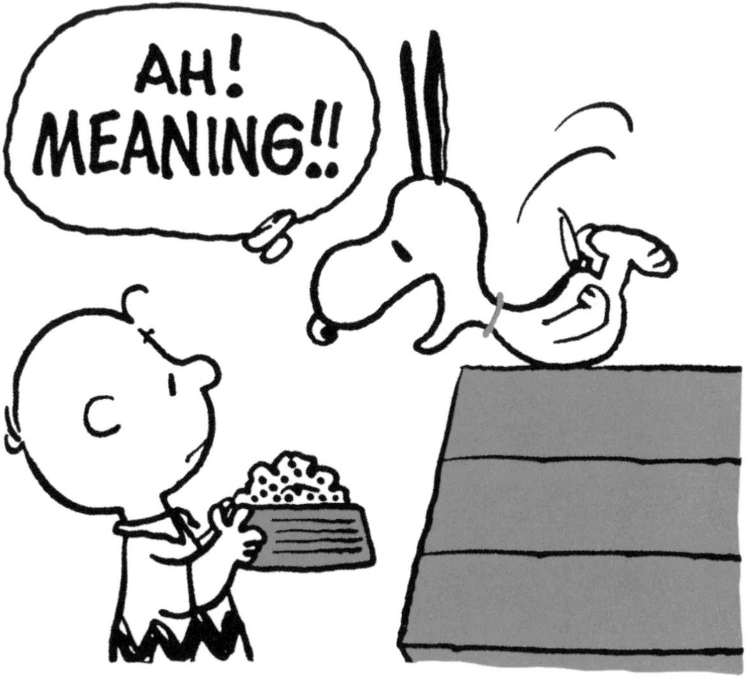
AH! MEANING!!

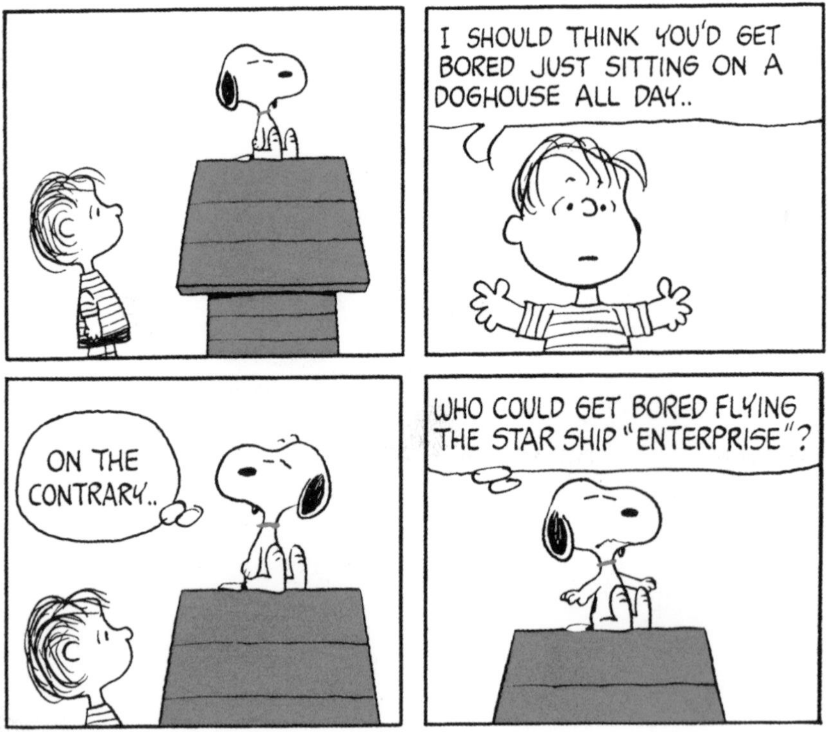
I SHOULD THINK YOU'D GET BORED JUST SITTING ON A DOGHOUSE ALL DAY..
ON THE CONTRARY..
WHO COULD GET BORED FLYING THE STAR SHIP "ENTERPRISE"?

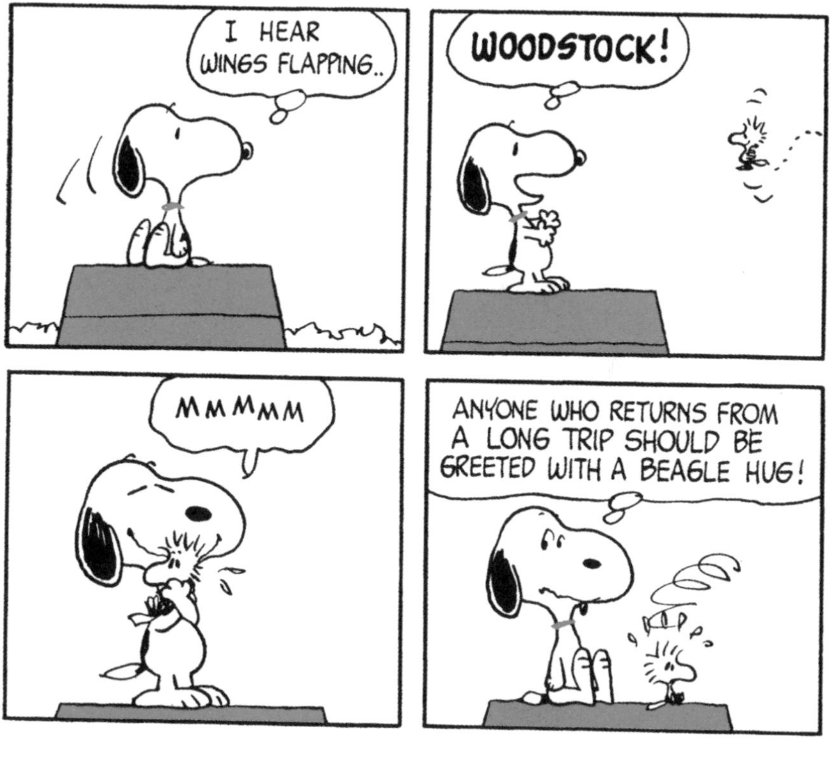
I HEAR WINGS FLAPPING..
WOODSTOCK!
MMMMM
ANYONE WHO RETURNS FROM A LONG TRIP SHOULD BE GREETED WITH A BEAGLE HUG!

RATS..I'M STILL HUNGRY..
MAYBE I CAN GET AN ADVANCE ON TOMORROW NIGHT'S DINNER..
ANOTHER ADVANCE?
YOU ARE NOW FIVE YEARS AHEAD OF YOURSELF ON DINNERS!

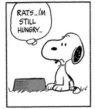

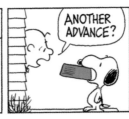

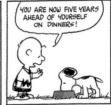

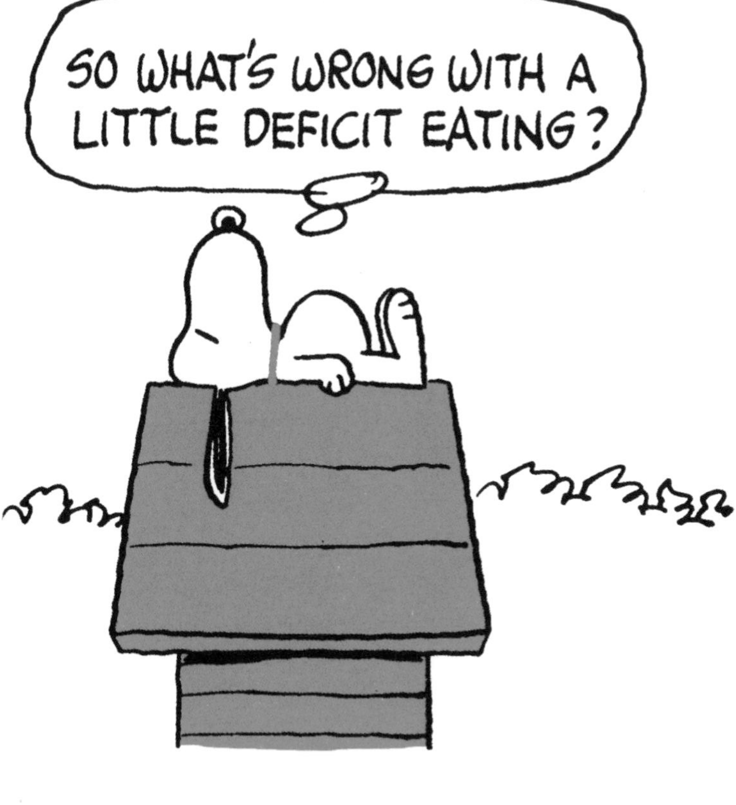
SO WHAT'S WRONG WITH A LITTLE DEFICIT EATING?

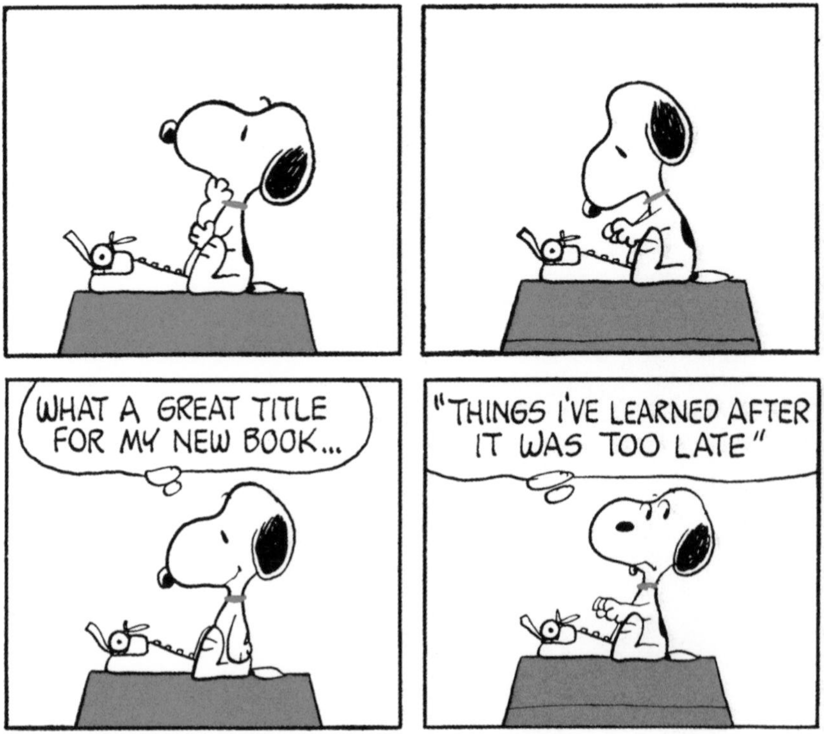
WHAT A GREAT TITLE FOR MY NEW BOOK...
"THINGS I'VE LEARNED AFTER IT WAS TOO LATE"

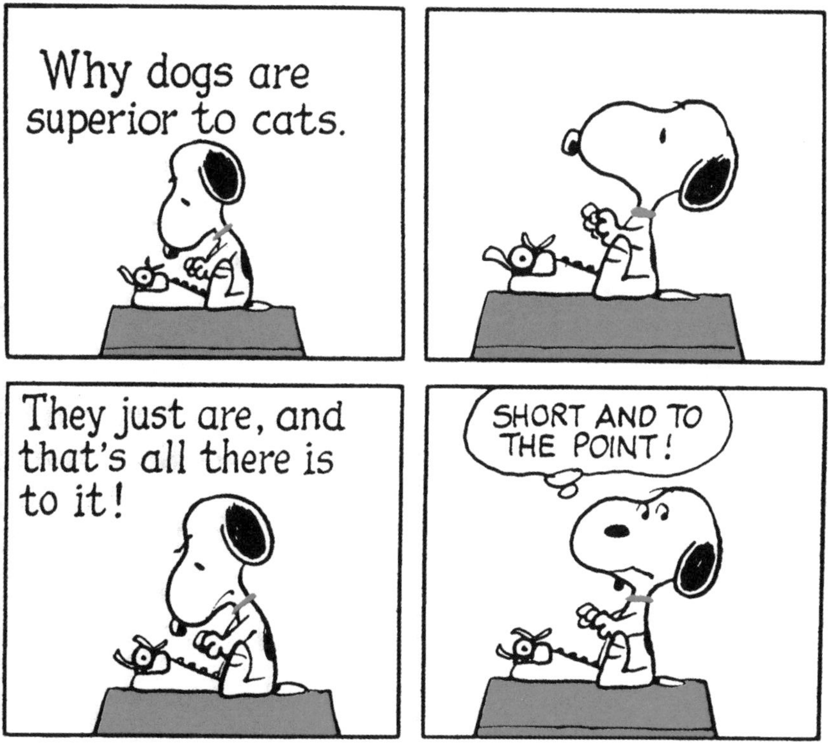
Why dogs are superior to cats.
They just are, and that's all there is to it!
SHORT AND TO THE POINT!

TODAY FOR "SHOW AND TELL" I HAVE BROUGHT MY BROTHER'S DOG...

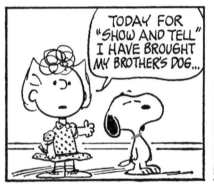

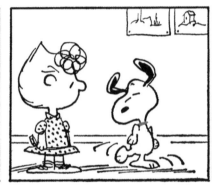

WHICH MAY TURN OUT TO BE THE BIGGEST MISTAKE OF MY LIFE!

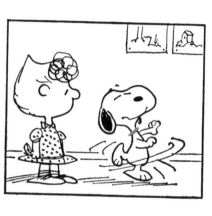

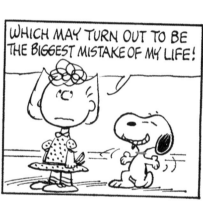

FORGET IT!

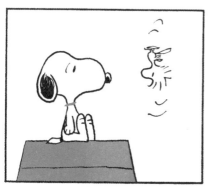

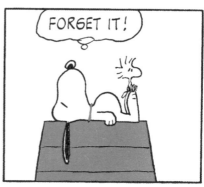

"I FOUND MY SISTER BELLE... AND WHAT A REUNION WE'RE HAVING! BELLE IS JUST AS BEAUTIFUL AS EVER"
"UNFORTUNATELY, I CAN'T SAY MUCH FOR HER TEEN-AGE SON"

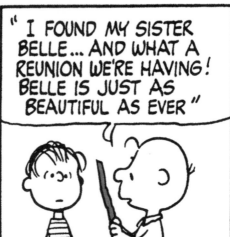

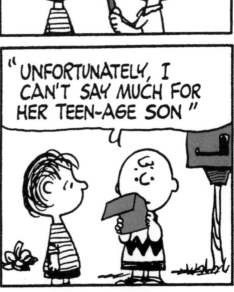

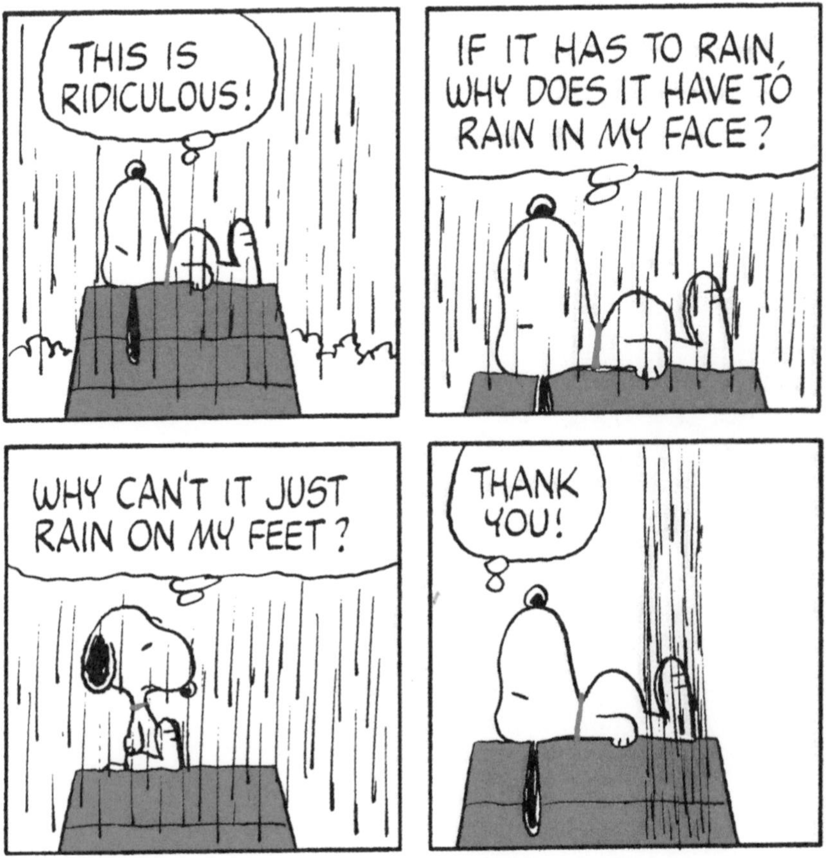
THIS IS RIDICULOUS!
IF IT HAS TO RAIN, WHY DOES IT HAVE TO RAIN IN MY FACE?
WHY CAN'T IT JUST RAIN ON MY FEET?
THANK YOU!

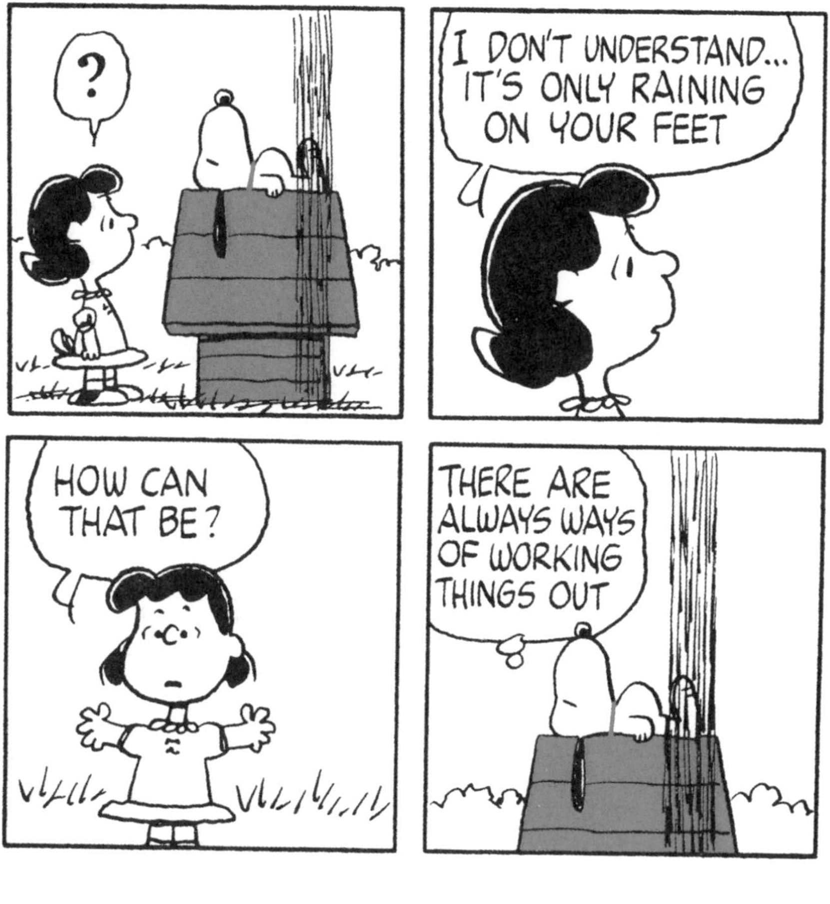
?
I DON'T UNDERSTAND... IT'S ONLY RAINING ON YOUR FEET
HOW CAN THAT BE?
THERE ARE ALWAYS WAYS OF WORKING THINGS OUT

I NEED A VACATION
BY GOLLY, I'M GOING TO PACK UP AND LEAVE!
I CAN SEE ME NOW LYING ON SOME BEAUTIFUL BEACH, SOAKING UP THE SUN..

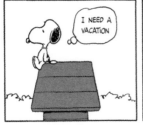

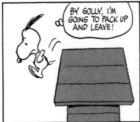

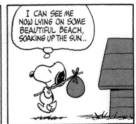

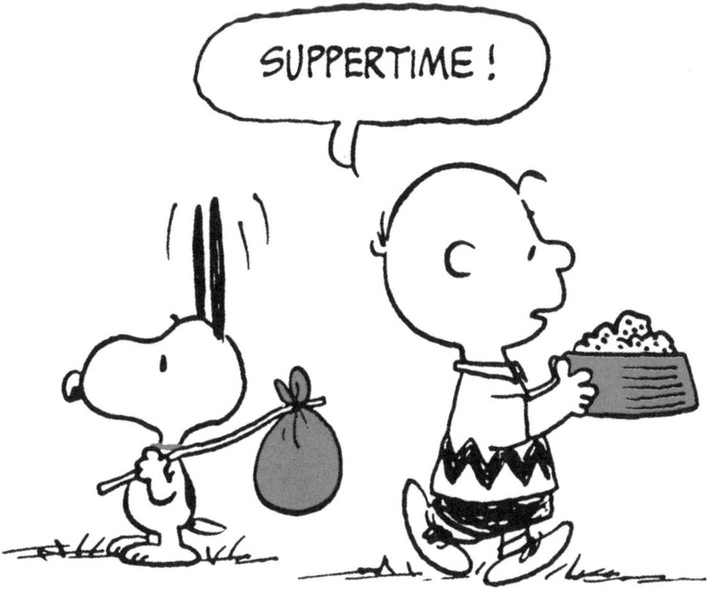
SUPPERTIME !

IT'S A LONG WAY TO...

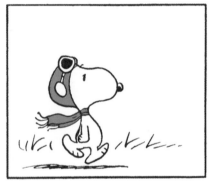

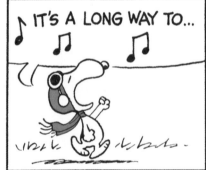

TIPPERARY
1 Block
SIGH

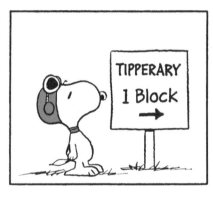

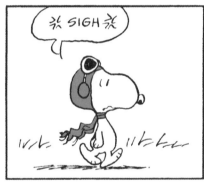

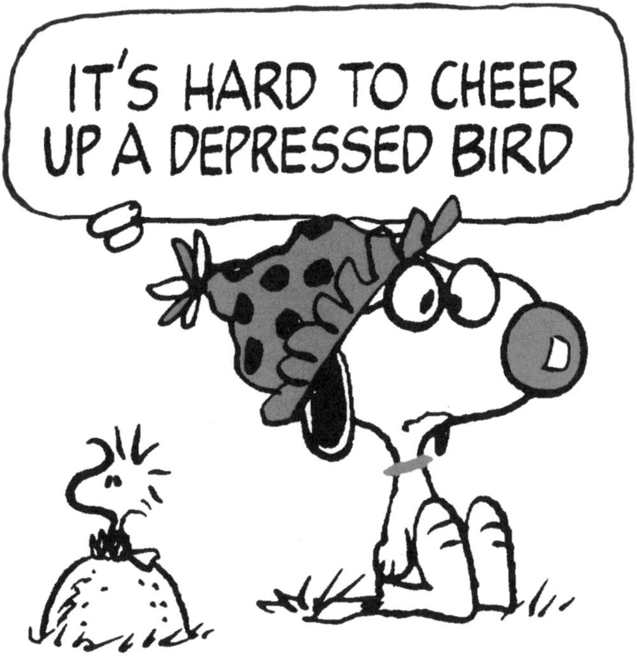
IT'S HARD TO CHEER UP A DEPRESSED BIRD

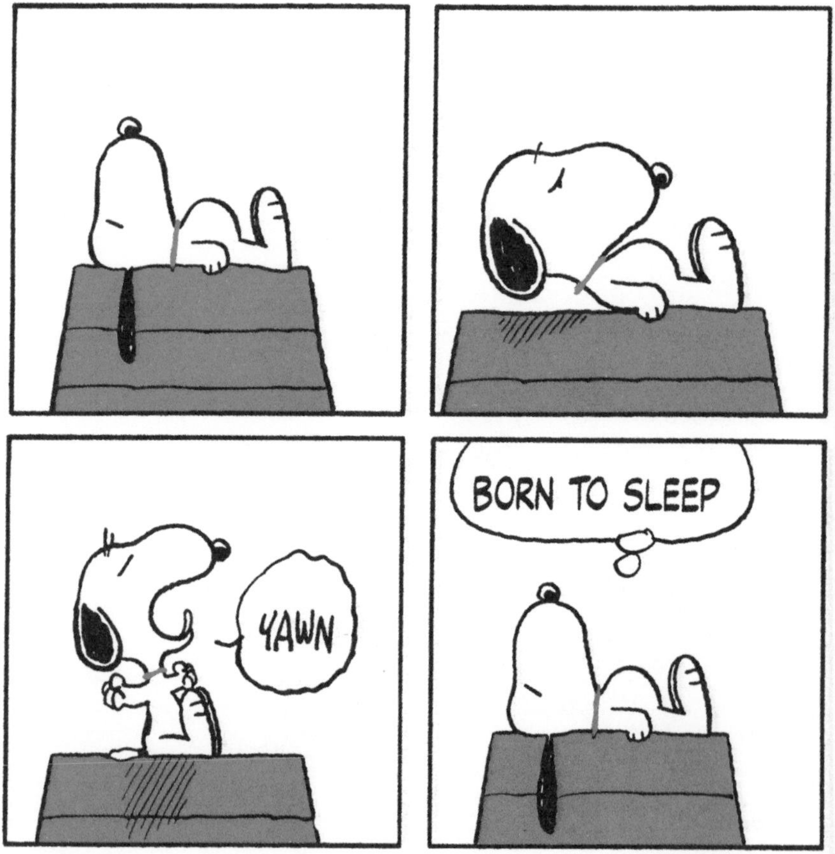
YAWN
BORN TO SLEEP

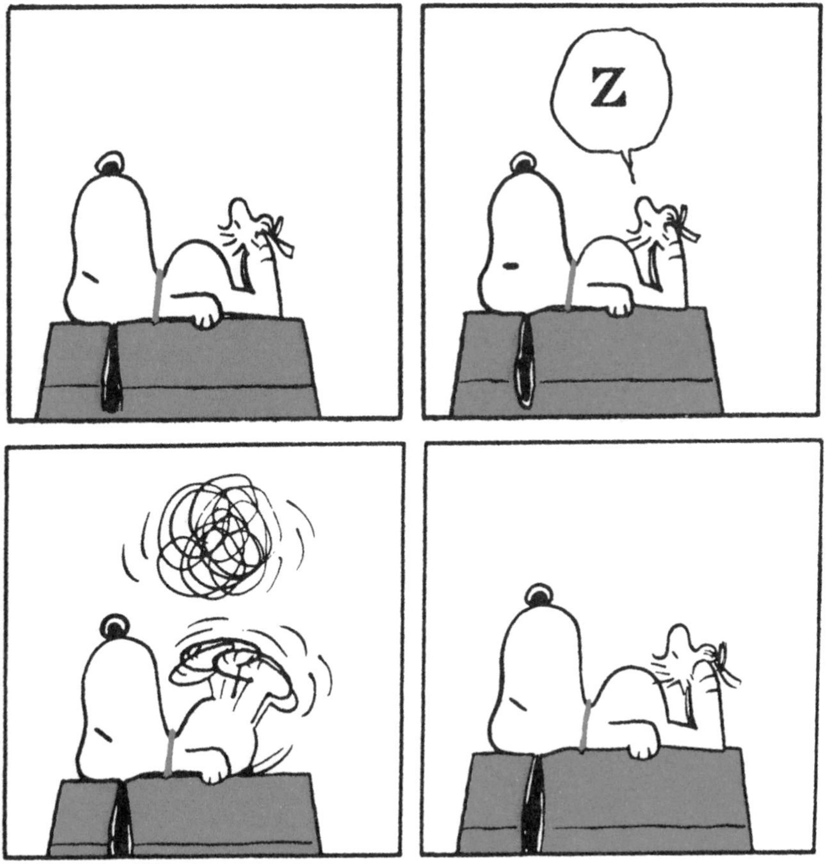
Z

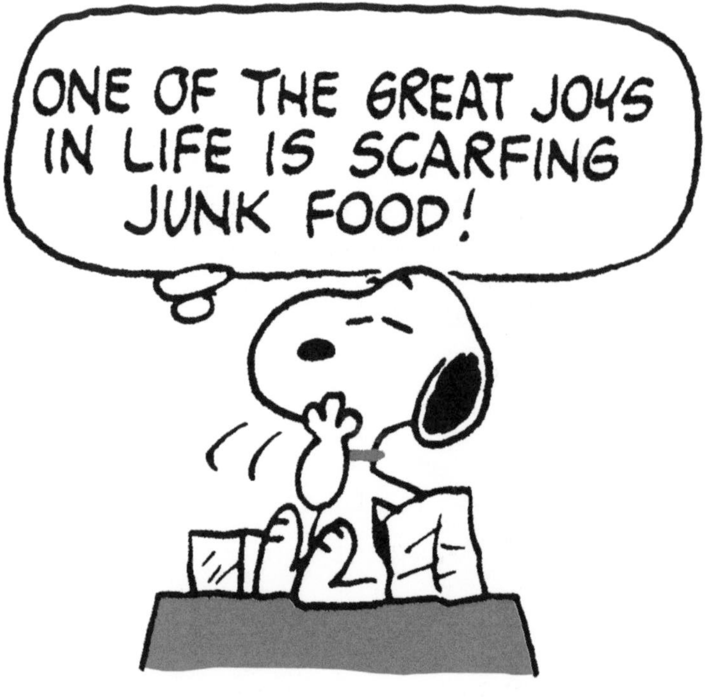
ONE OF THE GREAT JOYS IN LIFE IS SCARFING JUNK FOOD!

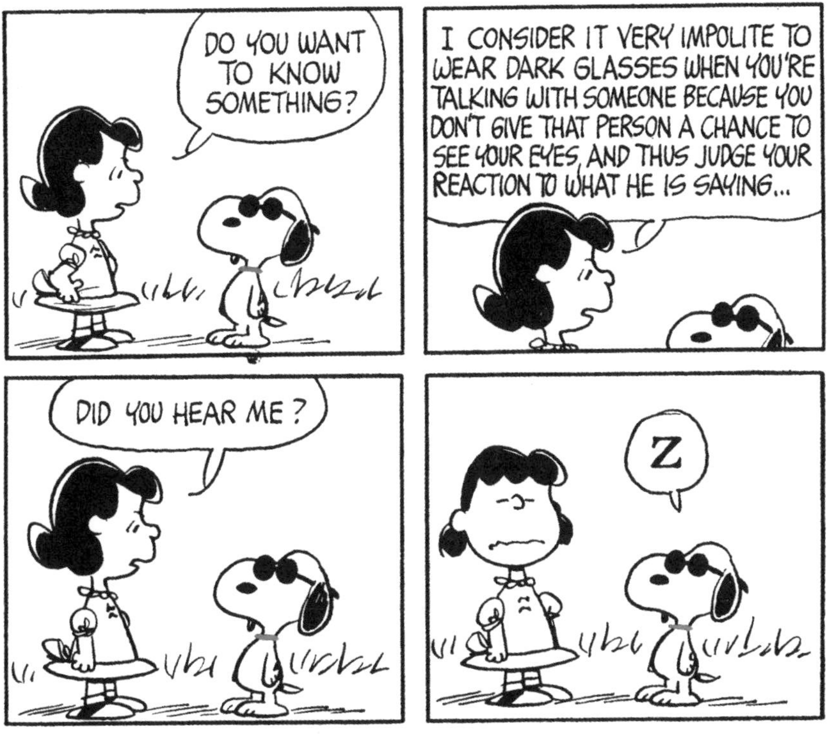
DO YOU WANT TO KNOW SOMETHING?
I CONSIDER IT VERY IMPOLITE TO WEAR DARK GLASSES WHEN YOU'RE TALKING WITH SOMEONE BECAUSE YOU DON'T GIVE THAT PERSON A CHANCE TO SEE YOUR EYES, AND THUS JUDGE YOUR REACTION TO WHAT HE IS SAYING...
DID YOU HEAR ME?
Z

HERE'S JOE COOL HANGING AROUND THE DORM
RING RING
RING RING RING RING

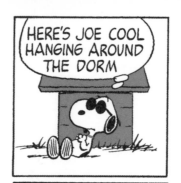

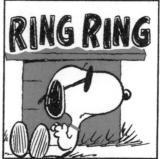

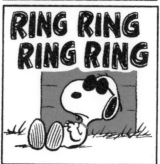

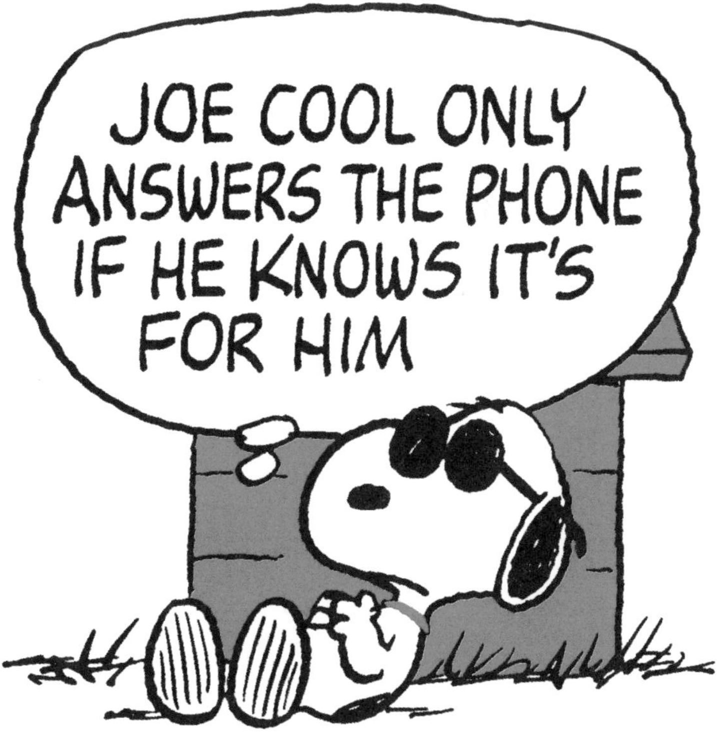
JOE COOL ONLY ANSWERS THE PHONE IF HE KNOWS IT'S FOR HIM

HERE'S JOE COOL HANGING AROUND THE DORM...
JOE COOL ALWAYS KEEPS UP WITH THE LATEST CAMPUS FADS...

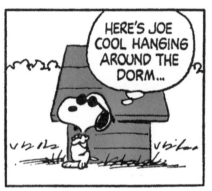

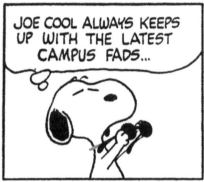

AND WHAT'S THE LATEST CAMPUS FAD?
STREAKING!!!

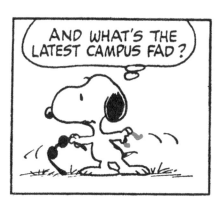

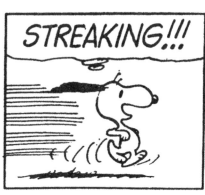

Dear Contributor,
We regret to inform you that your manuscript does not suit our present needs. The Editors

STOMP! STOMP! STOMP! STOMP!

P.S. Don't take
it out on your
mailbox.

SLEEPING AGAIN
I DON'T SEE WHY YOU NEED SO MUCH REST

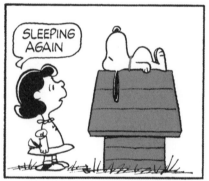

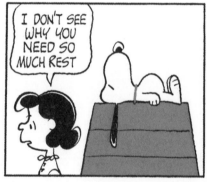

I NEED PLENTY OF REST IN CASE TOMORROW IS A GREAT DAY..
IT PROBABLY WON'T BE, BUT IF IT IS, I'LL BE READY!

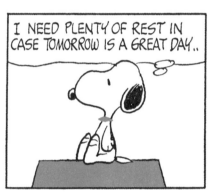

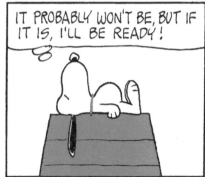

DO YOU EVER FEEL LIKE RUNNING AWAY?
OF COURSE... SOMETIMES I FEEL LIKE I WANT TO RUN AWAY FROM EVERYTHING

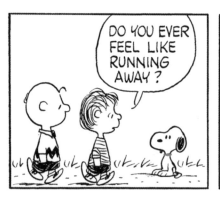

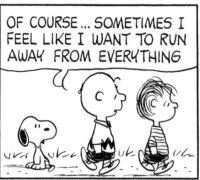

I REMEMBER HAVING THAT FEELING ONCE WHEN I WAS AT THE DAISY HILL PUPPY FARM..

I CLIMBED OVER THE FENCE, BUT I WAS STILL IN THE WORLD!

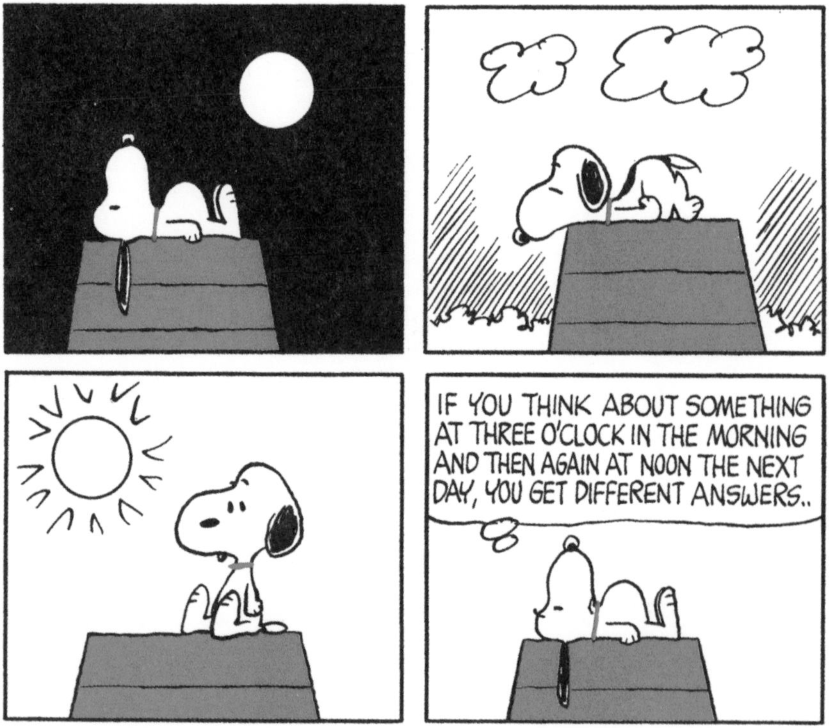
IF YOU THINK ABOUT SOMETHING AT THREE O'CLOCK IN THE MORNING AND THEN AGAIN AT NOON THE NEXT DAY, YOU GET DIFFERENT ANSWERS..

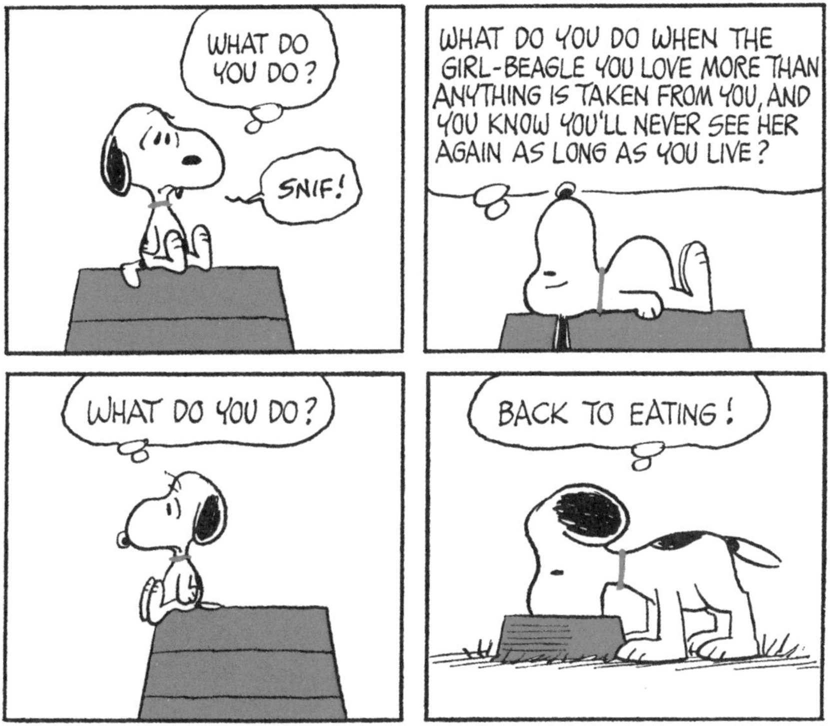
WHAT DO YOU DO?
SNIF!
WHAT DO YOU DO WHEN THE GIRL-BEAGLE YOU LOVE MORE THAN ANYTHING IS TAKEN FROM YOU, AND YOU KNOW YOU'LL NEVER SEE HER AGAIN AS LONG AS YOU LIVE?
WHAT DO YOU DO?
BACK TO EATING!

HERE'S THE WORLD WAR I FLYING ACE BEING CHASED BY THE RED BARON...
HE HATES ME!

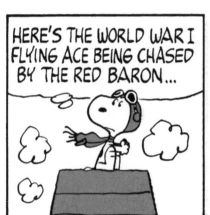

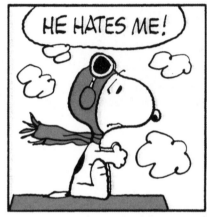

EVERYONE ASKS HOW I KNOW HE HATES ME...
I CAN TELL!

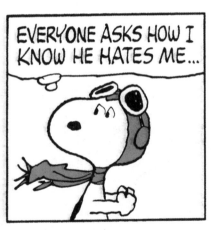

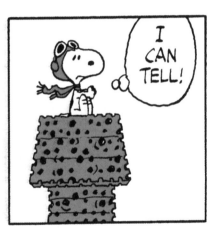

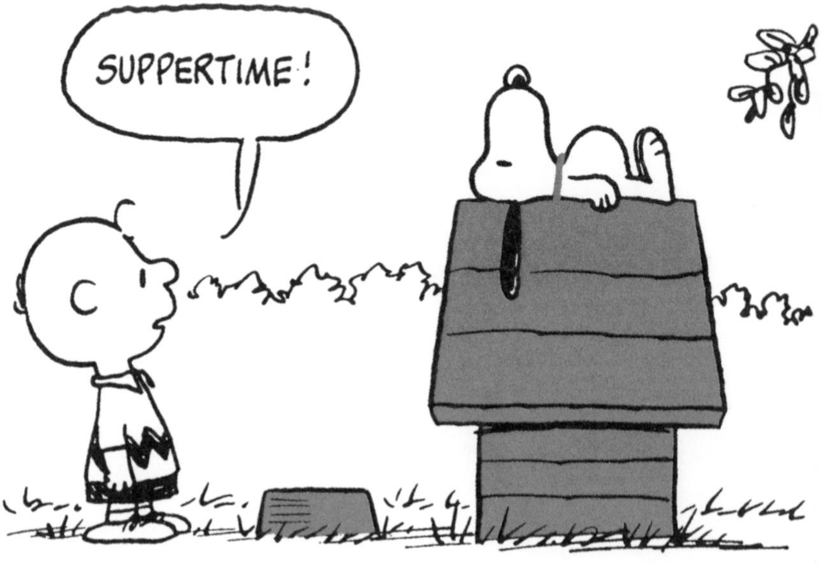
SUPPERTIME!

THANK YOU
YOU DON'T GET A TIP FOR CARRYING IN YOUR OWN DISH!

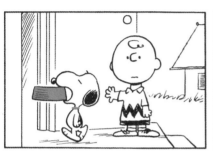

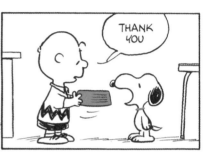

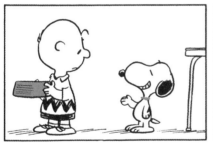

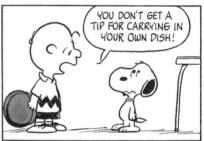

HAVE YOU EVER KNOWN ANYONE WHO WAS HAPPY?

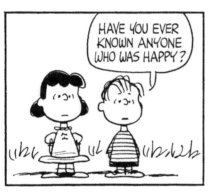

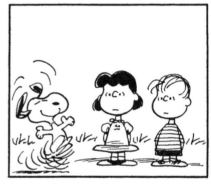

SMAK
AND WAS STILL IN HIS RIGHT MIND, I MEAN..

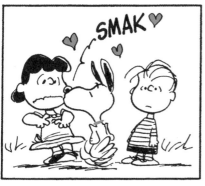

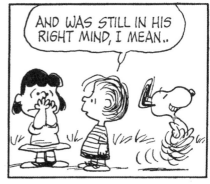

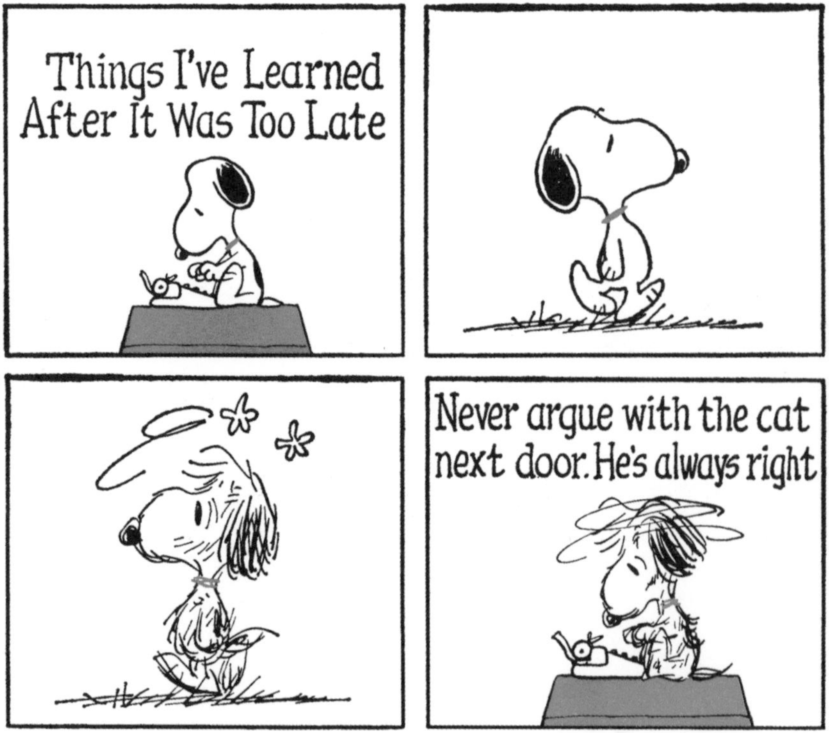
Things I've Learned After It Was Too Late
Never argue with the cat next door. He's always right

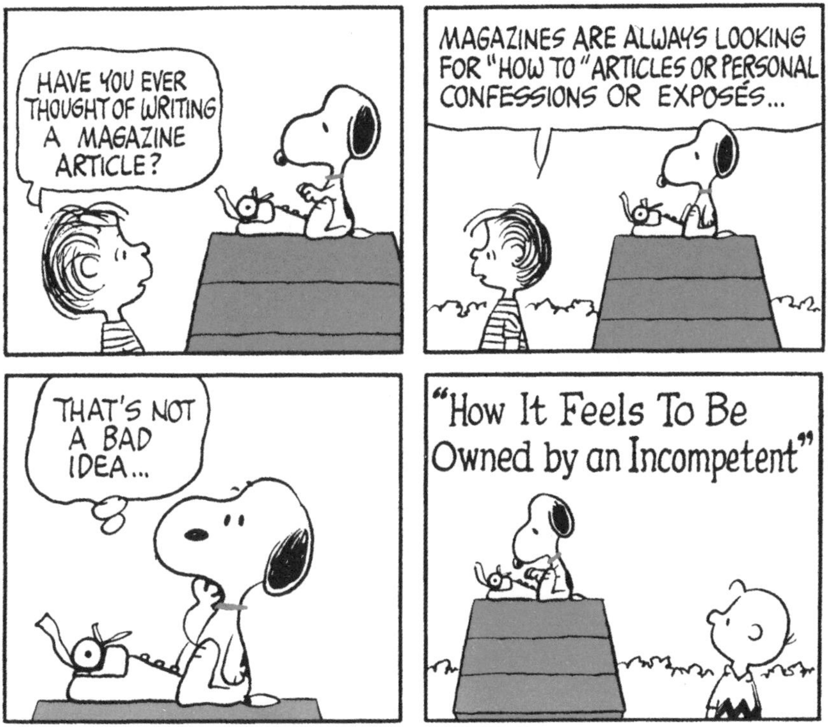
HAVE YOU EVER THOUGHT OF WRITING A MAGAZINE ARTICLE?
MAGAZINES ARE ALWAYS LOOKING FOR "HOW TO" ARTICLES OR PERSONAL CONFESSIONS OR EXPOSÉS...
THAT'S NOT A BAD IDEA...
"How It Feels To Be Owned by an Incompetent"

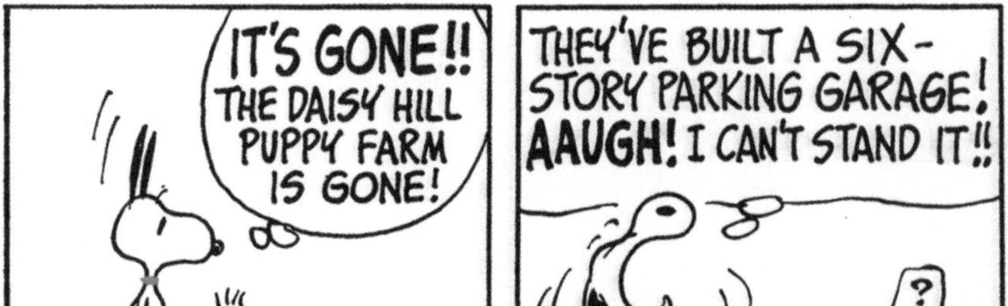
IT'S GONE!! THE DAISY HILL PUPPY FARM IS GONE!
THEY'VE BUILT A SIX-STORY PARKING GARAGE! AAUGH! I CAN'T STAND IT!!
?

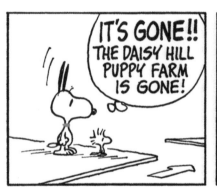

YOU STUPID PEOPLE!!
YOU'RE PARKING ON MY MEMORIES!!!

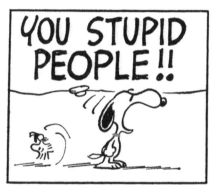

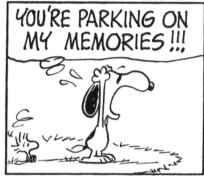

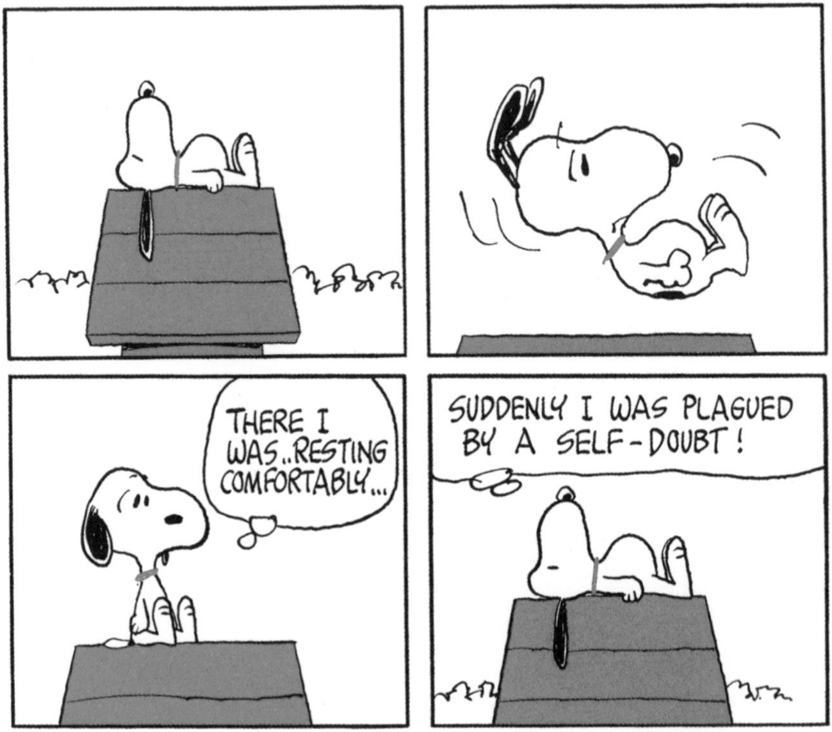
THERE I WAS..RESTING COMFORTABLY...
SUDDENLY I WAS PLAGUED BY A SELF-DOUBT!

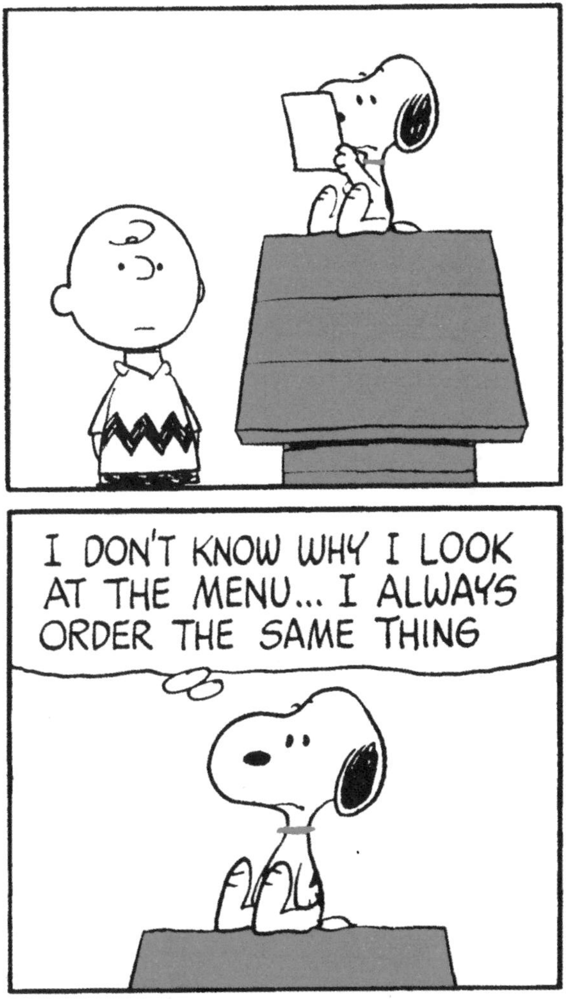
I DON'T KNOW WHY I LOOK AT THE MENU... I ALWAYS ORDER THE SAME THING

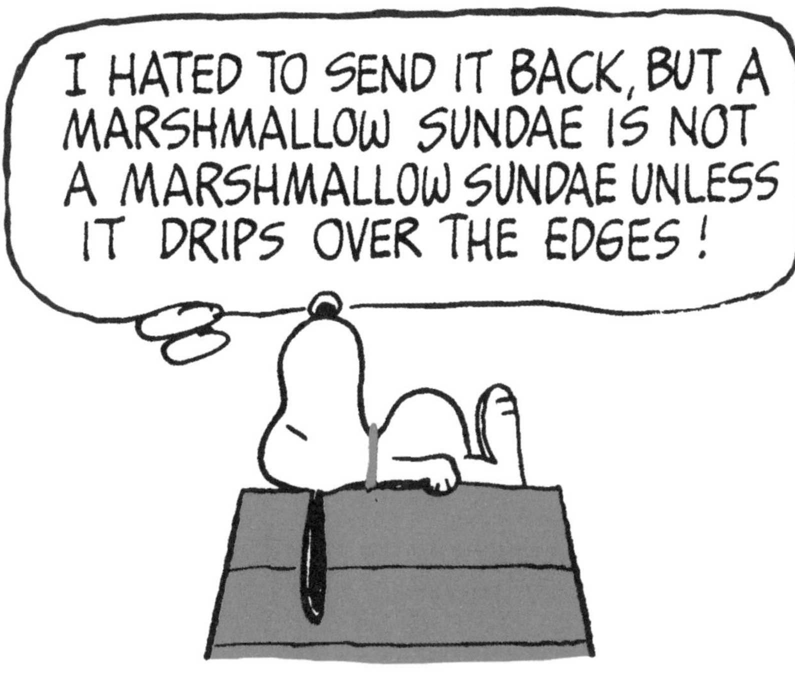
I HATED TO SEND IT BACK, BUT A MARSHMALLOW SUNDAE IS NOT A MARSHMALLOW SUNDAE UNLESS IT DRIPS OVER THE EDGES!

LEARN FROM YESTERDAY
LIVE FOR TODAY

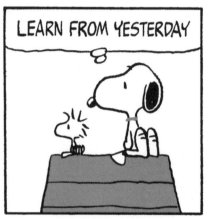

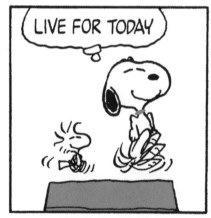

LOOK TO TOMORROW
REST THIS AFTERNOON

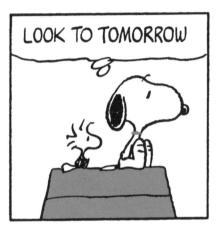

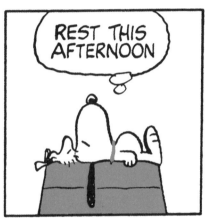

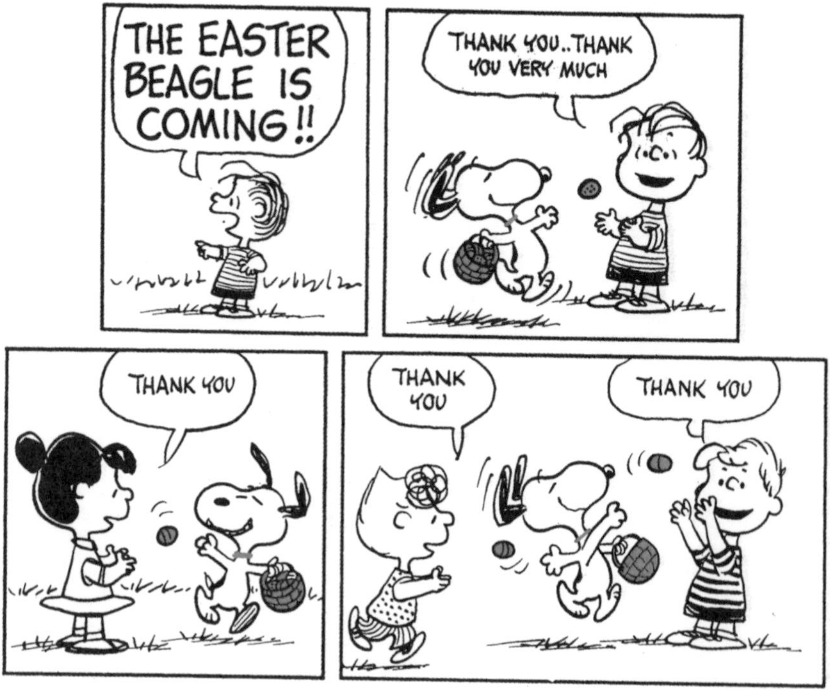
THE EASTER BEAGLE IS COMING!!
THANK YOU..THANK YOU VERY MUCH
THANK YOU
THANK YOU
THANK YOU

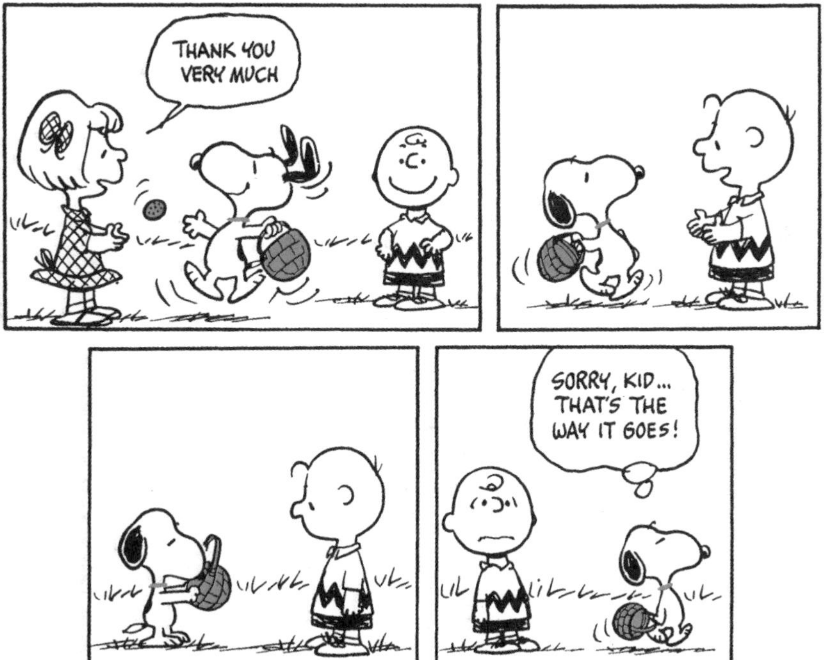
THANK YOU VERY MUCH
SORRY, KID... THAT'S THE WAY IT GOES!

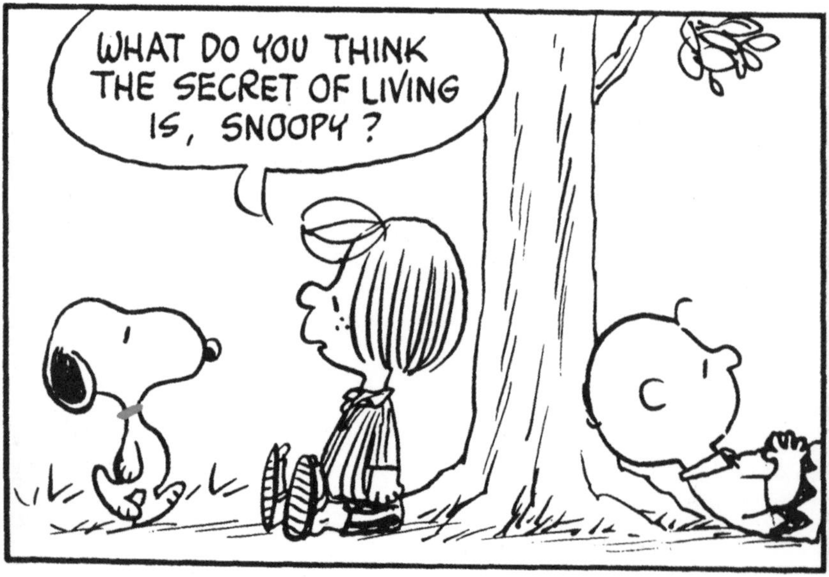
WHAT DO YOU THINK THE SECRET OF LIVING IS, SNOOPY ?

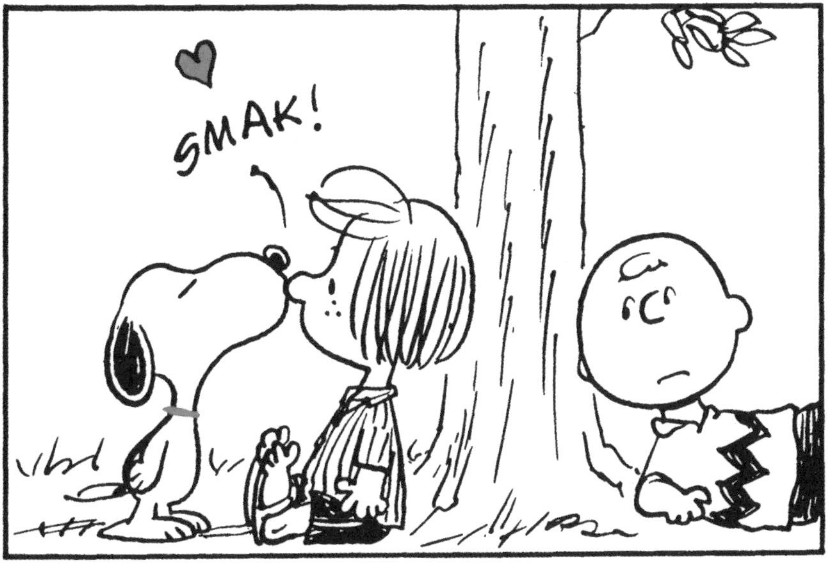
SMAK!

BOOKS AREN'T
EVERYTHING!

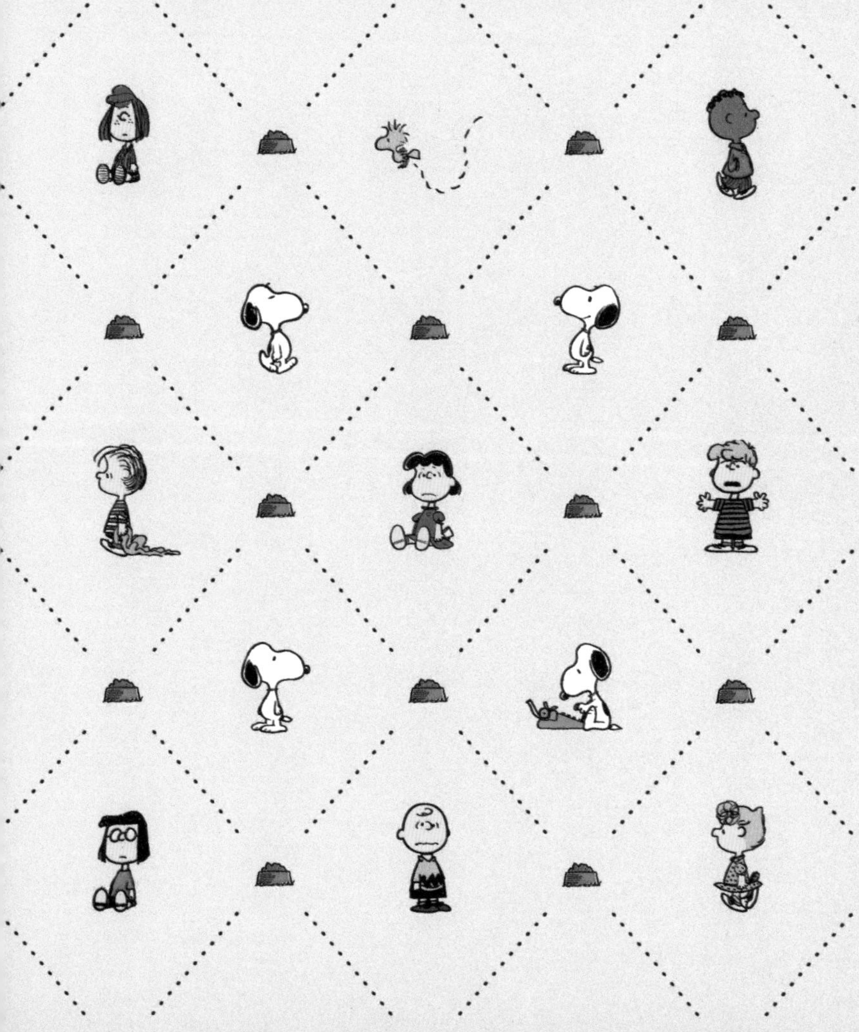

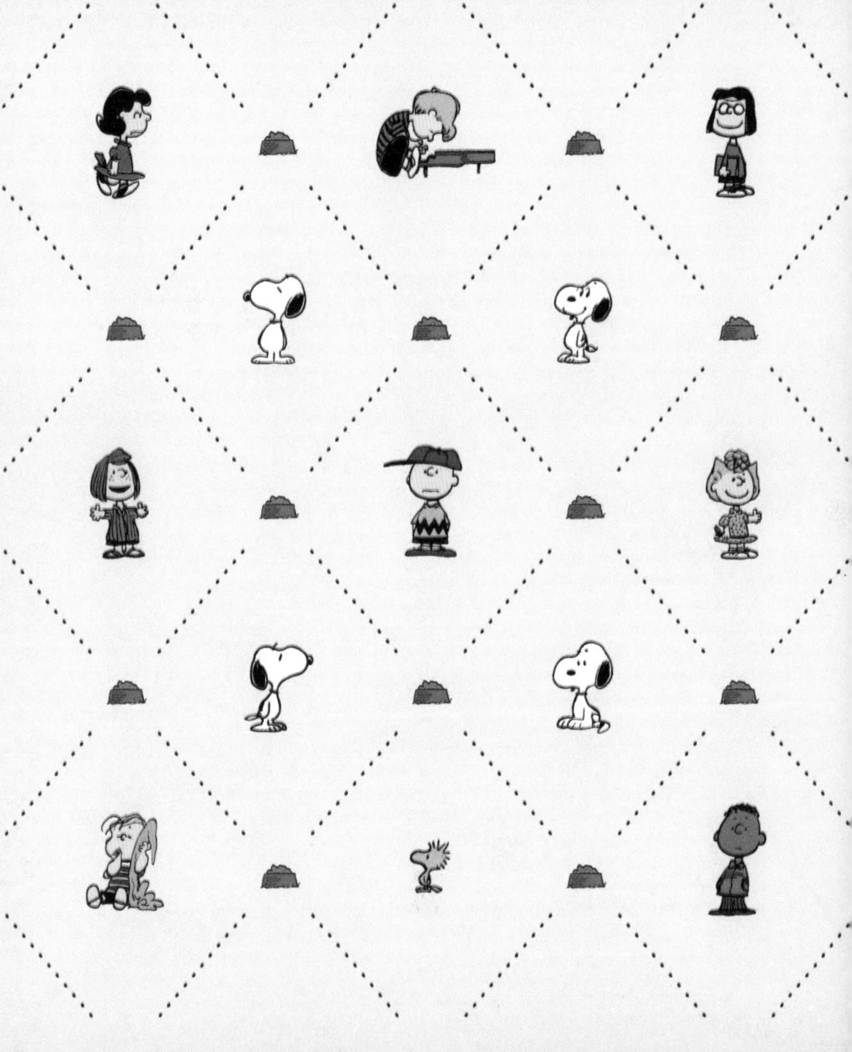